Symptômes

Gabriella Maione is a French playwright, director and actress, born and raised in Italy and currently living in New York. As an actress she has worked with Luis Buñuel in the Oscar-winning Best Foreign Language Film *The Discreet Charm of the Bourgeoisie*, and with Pier Paolo Pasolini in *The Decameron*. Her directing of Heiner Müller's *Quartett* at the Brooklyn Academy of Music received critical acclaim in 2001. *Symptômes* is her first published play.

T0258371

This page intentionally left blank

Gabriella Maione

Symptômes

translated by the author

Methuen Drama

Published by Methuen Drama 2007

1 3 5 7 9 10 8 6 4 2

Methuen Drama
A & C Black Publishers Limited
38 Soho Square
London W1D 3HB
www.acblack.com

ISBN: 978 1 408 10392 0

A CIP catalogue record for this book is available
from the British Library.

Typeset by Country Setting, Kingsdown, Kent

At time of going to press, *Symptômes* was due to premiere at Teatr Dramatyczny in Warsaw, Poland, on 27 November 2007 in a production by Teatr Dramatyczny, Change Performing Arts and RPN Globe LLC. Cast details were not confirmed.

Performed by the company of Teatr Dramatyczny

Direction, set design and lighting concept by Robert Wilson
Music by Michael Galasso
Dramaturg Ellen Hammer
Costume design by Michael Cepress
Lighting design by A. J. Weissbard
Collaboration to set design by Serge von Arx with Raimund Voigt
Collaboration to stage direction by Sue Jane Stoker

This page intentionally left blank

Symptômes

Characters

Marie S.
The First Witness
The Second Witness
The Third Witness
The Man with the Telephone
Little Girl
Little Boy

Rest area of a belt highway around a metropolis.

A mountain of files, stage left, dominates the space.

Deafening noises of heavy trucks mix occasionally with the mechanical rhythm of a giant printing machine.

The steady beat of a marching army underscores, contrapuntally, Gregorian chants, the sharp call of a muezzin, or the threnody from a synagogue.

Marie S. *enters, forcing a path through the papers.*

Marie S.
Who would have suspected that the Trojan horse
had given birth to quadruplets
and its unbridled sons
blindfolded winged Centaurs
had spouted their incandescent steel
over the sated sleep of the ignorant . . .
Inconceivable geographic slippage
bloodthirsty sacrilege
slaves' red outrage
dared against the omnipotent blue sky
of the indispensable CITY . . .
Vertical, unassailable city
which we saw for one instant fall to its knees . . .

The Three Witnesses *arrive from opposite directions.*

The Three Witnesses (*one after the other*)
That happened
that really
really happened . . .
SCHULD . . . SCHULD . . .
Fault . . . Debt . . .

Marie S.
The steel outrage
bloody, irreversible
for ever more contaminates earth and heaven
and the Event endures
and demands a reckoning

of the City's loss of affect . . .
How, after that, can you hold dear
your collective anaesthesia
stunted certainties
the Snakes and Ladders
of the newborn century . . .
TRAGEDY has returned
its backwards step blazing
along the path of omens . . .
it had long deserted
the retreating phalanxes of History
hurling the Globe into Lethe's arms . . .
LETHE, Eros' hot minion . . .
That all happened . . .
that all really happened . . .
Not one of those end-of-millennium
biblical sores
or those
theatrical warmongerings
the narcissistic effusion
of democratic dictators . . .
but the epiphany of CHAOS
the twilight of OMNIPOTENCE
the resurrection of UTOPIA
which PRACTICE had devoured . . .
And the whys break
from the sewn lips
and the hows break
from the straw-stuffed brains
and the soul breaks
from the palaces where she dwells . . .
For what
for whom . . .
As if an answer
were conceivable . . .

The Three Witnesses
The answer
is the cursing of the question

for the question
is the torturer of the answer . . .

Marie S.

Listen, O listen . . .
The sirens of revenge
fling forth their songs of torment
from the stultifying screens of the world . . .
Once again Violence seizes
its archaic designs for hegemony run amok . . .
Cemeteries of candles
burn their opalescent tears
on the alarmed asphalt of the cities . . .
War with its bloodied boots
has taken up office in the Capitol . . .

The First Witness

Inexplicable events
prowl the cities
like lost dogs . . .

The Second Witness

And there are no more eyes
seeking eyes . . .

The Third Witness

And there are no more fingers
pointing the finger . . .

The First Witness

And there is no more shelter
to shelter beneath . . .

The Second Witness

Is it on account of
the places that are evil-erected
and remain invisible . . .

The Third Witness

Or is it the fratricidal ferment
to occupy the
Highest Hall . . .

The First Witness
Or is it thanks to an aborted closing argument
for the liberation of the planets . . .

The Second Witness
Or is it because of ignorance
with respect to the roots of ignorance . . .

The Third Witness
Or else, from absence of regard
for the law of blood
or the law of the soil
the hell-bent law
of bloody flags and shrouds . . .

The First Witness
Or else is it
for having mistreated as bastards
the children of the Prophet . . .

Marie S.
That happened
that really happened . . .
Whereas I
doubly bloodied
doubly dumb
doubly responsible
escapee . . . survivor . . .
no longer resisting
the temptation to resist
yes, I, would I have submitted
merely to speak of nothing but Murder . . .

The First Witness
Who knows . . . who might know it . . .
'*Falaktahama l'aakabah ouamma adraqa malaahkabah* . . .
If only you knew what is the rocky pass
The freeing of a slave
Or feeding, upon a day of famine
An orphan near of kin' . . .

Marie S.

    Was it on a libertine
    whim for Utopia
    that I managed to withdraw
    those sealed documents
    those blood-soaked papers
    those felonious letters . . .
    might this be
    my single memory . . .
    untraceable identity
    perilous imbroglio . . .

She picks up some papers, sarcastically.

    Compromising documents
    veritable time bombs . . .
    There I am, entwined
    in the spirals of History
    flags over the coffins
    pernicious expectations . . .
    For here there might be
    the catapult that could blow up
    the Archives of the world
    above all those held by
    the Judaeo-Christian-Muslim Order
    alias the Abrahamic State Agency . . .
    It would be a scarlet carnival
    a black-and-white Bacchanal
    a verdigris Macro-happening . . .
    Si vis pacem, para bellum . . .
    Yes, if you love peace
    make ready for war . . .
    That is indeed how
    the riff-raff above
    get busy protecting
    human cattle . . .
    What, then, against these designs
    will we propose . . .
    Seeking here

the formula which would
blow up the Planet
or the secret reliquary
which in one instant
would put an end to War . . .
What are they trying to eradicate
with these hyper-technological thunders
pelting endlessly down
upon the sleeping cities . . .
This hue and cry . . . what's the good of it
how can I submit these eardrums
that love only
the backwash
of the Tyrrhenian Sea . . .
I have forgotten the crux
I sojourn at the crust
I have access just to details
to *nient'altro* . . .
were my crimes
so risible . . .

The Three Witnesses
Be calm, be impassive
be phlegmatic, be Olympian . . .
'Do not be afraid of your mistakes
thus you will make them into crimes' . . .

Marie S.
What asps have I warmed
between my breasts
what alliances have I smothered
between my thighs . . .
Was the function that was mine
in the unassailable city
so misshapen . . .
Was it to articulate
the Prince's discourse
to feed the voice of the white Male
to choreograph his gestures
his techno-mystic executions

in the Colosseum of the Polis
I, the theatre devotee
envious of Anna Politkovskaya
jealous of Rosa Luxemburg, shot down on the snow . . .
I, the Eva Braun
I, the Condy ICE, with carnivorous smirk
I, the Elena Ceaușescu
I, the out of joint
I, the overreached . . .

Pause.

This intoxication is nevertheless titillating
everlasting, imperial . . .

The Three Witnesses
'To be sure, this is the way
to foil their preparations
and to crush their plans
beneath ridicule!' . . .

The Man with the Telephone
(*appearing at the top of the mountain*)
What the hell . . . right . . . You bet
I must hear out . . . be a good listener
Trust me . . . I'll be ALL EARS
You got here the merciless eavesdropper
I'll get this gal back in the box . . .

Marie S.
What does that intruder seek of me . . .
this is excessive . . .
Persephone abducted by Pluto . . .
Was he already on this site . . .
imperatively
he had no choice but to follow me . . .
My doppelgänger, my lightlessness . . .
Has he barged in to intercept
my existence, my quiddity
at the moment of accident
should I say incident

bifurcation
reversal
at that very moment
of unbridling
when the Event always knows
how best to copulate
with impressionable minds . . .

The Second Witness
She is lost, halfway along the path
like a little girl with white hair . . .

Marie S.
Losing the way
as one loses one's head . . .
SHOCK and AWE
KAPUT
as at the time of the TERROR
century's frivolous times
times of Republican Emperors
protégés of Hercules . . .
Would I have been a provost of bronze
an instigator of armed conflicts
a plantation house slave, a kapo
crudeness of smile . . . eyes without iris . . .
Atrocious premonition . . .
but memory is compassionate
now that the land of the Ancestors
is in the hands of minnows
in the fists of patriotists . . .
Would I thus have escaped from the Capitol . . .
Conscientious objector
State deserter . . .
It could cost you the memory of your own name
even to ignorance of yourself . . .
How many letters make up
the name assigned to me
and what does that masked 'M' utter
or, worse, that wiggly 'W'

embroidered with scarlet silk on this handkerchief . . .
Fabricated evidence . . .
Truth is oligarchic . . .
Alas . . . give me . . . give m—

The Third Witness

This is how at times
she would tonsure the Mighty
'Give me, I beg you, give me . . .
What then?
A second quiddity' . . .
Yet, for an avalanche of minutes
for an infinity of seasons and dawns
her mind has been held captive
by this single dream . . .

Marie S.

Can it be we are barefaced
vulnerable
without armour . . .
Is it possible . . .
Daughter of no man
she dreads the abyss
that haunts her origins . . .
A tarnished illusion, mirror of the name
abyss of NO . . . NICHT . . .
NIET . . . NEIN . . .

The Three Witnesses

It is as if she cried out
to dismiss fear
ÄÄOS . . . KODAUSCH . . . TABOU . . .
holy, consecrated, intangible . . .
disquieting, forbidden, impure . . .

The Man with the Telephone

Yes, sir, I got it . . . this is my job . . . To be tactical . . .
SECURITY IS HIERARCHICAL RESPECT
But . . . If I may, I would like, be forward-leaning . . .
I mean, not reflexive-pullback . . .

Marie S.

In what meander of grey matter
among what tragic brotherhood
has he gone to nestle
that rascal, that pharisee
of the Name . . . my NAME . . .
Or else must we first forget
to be free to remember again . . .

The Three Witnesses

The little pest
was asking us solemnly
what is that . . .
why have old people
chosen to be old . . .

Marie S.

My parts . . . I am a part . . .
Becoming part . . .
I am coming I am coming
coming back whole . . .
What happens
it is not
everything we forget . . .

The Three Witnesses

It is as if she
confessed to herself
like the adolescent poet
'I was I
whereas today
I is another' . . .

Marie S.

LETHE, Oblivion
companion of Eros . . .
These breasts reveal
my belonging
to the *sexus sequior*, the second sex
as well as to the certainty
I have been stripped of rank . . .

It was Napoleon who jested
'Women have no rank' . . .
Majesty, you may see I am well glad of it . . .
Women
'a sort of intermediary
between child and man' . . .
An INTERMEDIARY . . .
My word, that is Schopenhauer
falling in with the Corsican . . .
Might they be the godfathers
of this stolen mountain . . .
It is Napoleon's fault
It is Schopenhauer's feloniousness
It is Jefferson's incontinence
It is Nebuchadnezzar's faux pas . . .
What then was the plan
what did the Intermediary
try to conspire . . .

The Three Witnesses

Indeed it's true to life . . .
'My memory, sir
is like a garbage-heap' . . .
It is as though she inflamed the Earth
'*Incede quod adorasti*'
burn what you love . . .
Thus spake Bishop Rémy
one day to Clovis . . .

The Man with the Telephone

Mark my words . . . this has highest intelligence value . . .
It's fishy, outrageous, vicious
It's cursing the National Agenda . . .
She looks neither right nor left . . .

Marie S.

How better to brandish
those documents withdrawn
from the cities slumbering
on the jointly committed Crime . . .

Dog-eared, yellowed papers
dazzled rats abandoning their coffers
bruised trees longing for the forest . . .
the world's devouring past . . .
Papyrus . . . Papieren . . . Daguerreotypes . . .
unsuspected, intolerable
often bestowed with
a harrowing obscenity
similar to this gross-bellied
inadmissible case
holding images of how to violate
international rights . . .
Sometimes they decree
as if they ruled
prior to the disappearance of Vespasian . . .
Is it a matter of a *coup d'état* . . .
Or else, would they get ready
to serve the sons
as their mother's meal . . .

The First Witness

Vespasians, those public urinals
funerary monuments
where confiscated-sex
ex-men
keep their eyes low
over the ammoniac steam
of their bodily water . . .

Marie S.

Public reading rooms to the four winds
street urinals of love
brothel-latrines
armours of lapping liquids and rust . . .
How many *Homo sapiens*
could they hold without exploding
clammy bellies bumping into each other
at the ultimate gate of a beloved . . .
Lust lavatory
sour spaces of ammonia

and penumbra . . .
Body to body in a lonely clinch to the heart
weeping flesh laid open
to the ultimate pleasure . . .

The Three Witnesses

In the middle of international summits
she made a fool of them
paraphrasing Berthold . . .
My friends
if you want to see
something meaningful
then you may stop by a public Pissodrome . . .

Marie S.

In what year are we . . .
the angel of History
has suspended its utopian flights
that made dreamers of Europe's gentry . . .
These papers, burnt Icaruses . . .
Latin and German
Cyrillic and English
Farsi . . . even Pahlavi
hieroglyphics
cuneiform writing
Chuan Chu
ideograms
rupestrian drawings . . .
What then . . .
what is the meaning of this wonder
this deathly cattle fair
speaking the language
of the State Tarzan . . .
What is the strategy of the VULCANS
our emperor's limping blacksmiths . . .
Where has the other Pole of the earth
vanished to shatter . . .
The Globe has just traded in its curves
now it is naught but an anorexic Lolita
turned over to the drunkards

of fossil-fuel currency . . .
But Europe, maybe Europe can . . .

The Three Witnesses
Europe, alas, what can Europe do
that licentious aged matron . . .

Marie S.
Listen . . . make keen your ears
force yourself to penetrate . . .
Those words
are they not
the dirt of an alcoholic primate
a theomaniacal hominid
or a, a . . .

The Man with the Telephone (*on the mountain*)
This is fucking essential
We need a catastrophic
and catalysing event
Cartago delenda est . . .
The Commander-in-Chief
was paramount on that . . .
He said luminescently
'After all, this is the guy
who tried to kill my dad'
We are clear-cut about the guy
But now, motherfucker . . .
what the Hell we'll do
with this fucking cunt . . .

The Second Witness
You see . . .
In the cities with
transatlantic quarrels
they care only for keeping an erection . . .
They have a helluvan erection
in the cities
but they solely have erections
for the Tyrant . . .

Marie S.
This individual is pretending to communicate . . .
Fallacious . . . Pharisee . . . Jesuit . . .
Besides, they never like to exchange information . . .
are careful not to communicate
have a dispathy for each other
admit nothing crucial to each other
ply and play with Truth
are covetous, enraged
resentful, unsatisfied, rivals . . .
This is why they show suicidal solidarity . . .

The Three Witnesses
Might she be struggling to confide in us
'Truth is ugly
we have Art
so that the truth does not kill us' . . .

Marie S.
Pleasure is a weapon that suits us . . .
let's make a Mardi Gras of this end-of-the-world . . .
Let's raise oxygen . . .
Even slaves have a right to it . . .

The Three Witnesses
How can she take the liberty
of musing upon oxygen
aka, the holy GAS . . .
How dare she
covet raw materials
the august toys of the Emperor-Boy . . .

The Man with the Telephone
Can you believe it . . .
They gang up on oxygen . . .
on Artistic Gas . . .
Fucking fags and perverted . . .

Marie S.
To die, to leave, withdraw from life . . .
Expire, run dry from Art-deprivation . . .

And if we were to ruin THEM
by weaning them from art . . .
Let them sink in self-oblivion
as has befallen me . . .
weaning them for ever from their
hyperamnesia
hyperdynamia
hypertheomania . . .
Withdraw them from the stare
falling on us all
that 360-degree stare
turned upon us
from the HIGHEST HALL
the very one fantasized by Leibniz
at the tip of a pyramid
signifying the order of the world . . .

The Third Witness

One equals one
One hundred thousand billion equals
one hundred thousand billion . . .
In the cities
rife with cloning epidemics
they organize Oedipus group therapies . . .

Marie S.

DUMB SHOW
what can we do now
but act in a dumb show
toward a tragic future from a tragic past . . .
The Führerprinzip never died
cult of Il Duce
the angst of the nobodies . . .
Marx died from having dared to say
'Our goal is to be much
not to have much' . . .
Grim hubbubs
start up in the unbreathable air . . .
Grands dieux, à ces malheurs dois − je me préparer' . . .
'Great gods, must I ready myself for these misfortunes' . . .

In truth to prepare for the worst
might be the best we can get . . .
for straddling the crest of Chaos . . .

The Three Witnesses

Chaos is a whorehouse, a pigsty
a demolition site, higgledy-piggledy
a fuck-up, a dog's dinner
ass-backwards, diarrhoea, *la chaude-pisse* . . .

The Man with the Telephone

It's crystal clear . . . WMD . . .
RED ALERT . . .
ABRACADABRA . . . CONSPIRACY . . .
The supreme, ultimate Known Unknown . . .

Marie S.

No matter!
We shall convert chaos
into a poetry in motion
a stroke of luck . . .
O woe, horrific sacrifices
will be perpetrated
by insignificant hands . . .
War prisoners
faceless bodies
trophies of humiliated flesh
piled up in horrendous pyramids
asses, legs, sex exposed
to the orgasmic flash
of the redemptory militia . . .
In truth, nothing has changed . . .
monsters . . .
yes and no . . .
Cruelty sees its stocks push up
on the tumbled Market of Affects . . .

The First Witness

In the megalomaniac cities
there is no remission for sinners . . .
They weep, crown of thorns

in the style of Caesar at thirty
reiterating broken-heartedly
'At my age, Alexander had already died' . . .

Marie S.

Guilty of that capital passion
risky collusion between self and self
this heinous pact to gain access
to the HIGHEST HALL . . .
Guilty thereafter of the piercing terror
of falling suddenly back down
the visceral, unspeakable panic
at the risk of being back naked in the arena . . .

The Three Witnesses

Ave Tiberius . . . Ave Caligula . . .
Ave Nero . . . Ave Domitiano . . .
Ave Commodus . . . Ave Caracalla . . .
Ave Heliogobalus . . . Ave Georgius Secundus
MORITURI TE SALUTANT
WE WHO ARE ABOUT TO DIE
SALUTE YOU . . .

Marie S.

They are Aristotle's slaves
those instruments gifted with speech
opposing at this fruitless instant
with their indignation
of the disinherited . . .
Plotting to implement
the *LEX TALIONIS* . . .

The Three Witnesses

Poor little us, we have caught her professing
'It is the slaves
who seize power and keep it
and in keeping it remain slaves' . . .

Marie S.

From what unravelled net
of a barbaric god

can those technological missionaries
have slipped out
to fling themselves at the head
of bloodthirsty armies . . .

The Second Witness
The Polis huffs and puffs
the gods are economical . . .
In the climbing city
indestructible
ramparts of garbage
arise without end
as protection from enemy phalanxes . . .

Marie S.
Like a wench
we shall fire up
IMAGINATION . . .
Those *URPHANTASIEN*
UR-phantasms
may they lend us a hand . . .

She murmurs.

'WHO? I REVOLT AGAINST A FATHER'S WILL?
AND DESERVE THE DEATH THAT I WOULD NOT
    FULFIL?
WHAT OF RESPECT? WHAT OF DUTY SUPREME?' . . .

The Man with the Telephone
(*shouting from the top of the mountain*)
Right, that's the question
what of respect
what of duty . . .
since that is what it's about, right?
OBEDIENCE and RESPECT, WHAT ELSE . . .

Marie S.
Can't you smell
a sickening odour
acrid, intolerable . . .
the smell of an open mass grave . . .

They are playing with human meat
each as much as the other . . .
No later than tonight
they announced a massive calamity
an attack organized in the minutest detail
something unheard of, never seen before . . .
It is for this very day
that those mugshots
these ephemeral cherry blossoms
are practising to extinguish the sun
to burn down the temple of Diana . . .
We are in the year 356 BC . . .
Erostratos wants to be immortal
even more than Alexander . . .
To set fire to Rome and watch it burn
Nero, tickling his lyre
weeps into his crystal vial . . .
I am God, because I make *TABULA RASA* . . .
Oh, list . . . Don't you hear
a deafening sound
a nuclear *RUMORE*
advancing with giant strides
something capable of making
the eardrums of the Earth explode . . .
Or else, this may be
an inhuman silence . . .
the silence holding up to us
its concave mirror of shadows . . .
For we are without eyes, without ears
confident in unsuspected exits
in inconceivable dawns . . .

The Three Witnesses

Do you remember
Ulysses' deadly threat . . .
'For yonder walls, that pertly front your town
your towers, whose wanton tops do buss the clouds
must kiss their own feet' . . .

The Man with the Telephone

(coming down from the mountain, orders)
YOU, YOU MUST KISS MY OWN FEET . . .

Marie S.

OK . . . MY OWN . . . why not . . . you, slow learner . . .
With the end of the world
it is imperative to cross the Rubicon . . .
No matter how alien to ourselves
how obliged for survival
to zigzag
under the fire of adolescent rifles . . .
. . . the Sniper at Large . . .
no matter how rocked
by this tedious wreckage
of commonplaces . . .
No matter if we must suffer
destruction and vanity
silliness and dishonour . . .
No matter . . .
Oderint dum metuant . . .

The Man with the Telephone

Right . . . we don't want
another fuck-up . . . OK
Fine, 'Let them hate us . . .
as long as they fear us' . . .

Marie S.

Confused . . . discombobulated . . .
asses . . . bottom of the class . . .
abused children . . . Snow Whites . . .
Let us begin to repeat
repeat all those texts and deed . . .
A chorus of children and old folk
of stutterers and happy liars
of tyrants and unlawful combatants
of gravediggers and false patriots
of believers and non-believers . . .

Pause.

I left everything behind
don't you remember, one day
the dreams, the threats
the deadly machines . . .

The Third Witness
You left everything behind one day . . .
cities with their endless terraces . . .
cities with their immortal dynasties . . .
cities where all is sea and stone and light . . .
cities that can be neither rebuilt nor remembered . . .

The Man with the Telephone
Quitting everything . . .
that is the FATAL SIN . . .

Marie S.
To repeat what has been written
by losing balance . . .
To repeat till the last breath
we, the beasts of burden
the public shame
the clowns
the carnies
the harlequins . . .
For a little actor
an actor doomed to the waiting room
a pathetic stage rabble-rouser
will know how to conjure
the absolute transgression . . .
'The storks wake no longer
in the meadows . . . '
At first
they will think of travelling
in tamed geographies . . .
classical authors . . .
classified threats . . .
And then . . . and then . . .
the familiar will become
more than flesh and blood can bear . . .

The First Witness
In the newborn cities
with raped landscapes
in the martyr hypo-cities
spattered with human flesh
the youngest fear
nothing but life . . .
On the ripped flag
of their hoodlum bodies
they tag with their blood
WE ARE
DYING
WHILE WE ARE
STILL ALIVE . . .

Marie S.
. . . so then the rabble above
will decide for the worse . . .
and with the worst
they will want us
panic-stricken, paralysed . . .
They mastermind a plan
to prevent us from
rehearsing tragedies . . .
They do it in a loving manner
with a masculine, compassionate
neoconservative graciousness . . .
See . . .

The Man with the Telephone
Right . . . their humane amiability
demon-cratic
militaro-cratic
speculo-cratic
lucre-cratic
sado-cratic . . .
You've got a problem with that . . .

Marie S.
There's something more . . .

The Man with the Telephone
Something else . . .

Marie S.
The statue of Justice . . .

The Man with the Telephone
Of Justice . . .

Marie S.
The bare-breasted one . . .
They commanded her covered . . .
with a blue flag
by order of the head of the Supreme Court . . .
The head of the Supreme Court
finds it condign to punish
this female nudity
Eve's sinful background
for his televised exhibitions . . .
blue velvet will take care of it . . .
They pester Racine
'Hide then that breast on which I cannot glance' . . .
On the cathode tube
the breast-phobic from the Bismarck State
allows no partner
firstly not female
chiefly not sporting
marble nipples . . .
God's lid . . .
I speak no treason . . .
That goddess blind
is in love
with the god of soldiers . . .

The Three Witnesses
'*Oua Koul li l mou amináti* . . .
Tell the believers to lower their eyes
to protect their sex . . .
May they pull their veils across their chests
may they show their attributes
solely to their husbands, to their fathers

to their fathers-in-law, to their sons
to their sons-in-law, to their brothers
to their slaves, to eunuchs
to pre-pubescent males' . . .

Marie S.

ICH BIN DIE BRUST . . .
I am the BREAST . . .
one of the last sentences
written by Sigmund . . .
and then
'The child so often lacks the breast' . . .
This lack of the breast
is lack of breath . . .

The Man with the Telephone

ICH BIN DIE BRUST
said the Episcopalian . . .

Marie S.

Would you be able to tell me
if in these ages
of apocalytic waiting
there is a lone living soul who might have
even the most approximate inkling
of what eroticism is . . .
someone indeed with
even the most myopic vision
of the sacred nature
of sexuality . . .

The Three Witnesses

The city associates the hindquarters
the bumper, the boiler room
the cooler, the cheeks
the buns, the fanny, the booty
the gluteus maximus
with Coca-Cola, Ex-Lax
Mutual Life
Roto-Rooter
toe fungus . . .

The Man with the Telephone
Yes, yes . . . right, right . . .
the BLOCKED TOE . . . I'm blocked . . .
I'm remorseful, but
I'm not cut out for pleasure . . .
I'm more in the style
of a matter-of-fact republican . . .

Marie S. (*coming very close to him*)
. . . What do you say . . .
do you want to play a little game . . .

The Man with the Telephone
What game?

Marie S.
A little game of war . . .
Look . . . look then . . .
You ought to . . .
Don't stop looking . . .
Would you dare turn away from this
suitable little garden . . .
this patio, you see . . . this dizzying aguedal . . .
this unreasonable precinct . . . this intemperate realm . . .
this untireable eden . . . this . . .
'Have no fear of inclining your face to this place' . . .

The Man with the Telephone (*as if in a trance*)
'Oh slit, oh sweet wet slit, dear giddy abyss . . .
Hail to thee, palace of rose, pale bower
honeycomb slightly undone
by the grave joy of love
vulva appearing in all its instant profusion' . . .

Marie S.
BRAVO . . . I am touched . . . tickled even . . .
However, you avowed yourself blocked . . .
you did say blocked, didn't you . . .
not cut out for pleasure . . .
Should I therefore take the liberty
of leading you three times into temptation
as the Nazarene was in the desert . . .

The Man with the Telephone
I am realistic . . . Right . . .
a re-a-list . . . at least . . . got it . . .
but what is essential
what is imperatively inseparable
from this here person
I am . . . realist–pragmatic–neocon . . .

Marie S.
Neocon . . .
your language is brutal . . .
your lexicon is a carrier of
philologico-cultural terrorism . . .
This is how your clique
would take measures to
excommunicate eroticism . . .
No matter . . .
your muzzled sensuality
seems to suffer from
such a heretical itch
that reveals a pathological intolerance
to State cunning . . . to cunt-servants . . .
Alas . . . their overhealthiness
seems to erode their orgasmic capacity . . .
That is the way
monsters arise . . .

The Three Witnesses
No one was paying attention
when she used to warn
'It is not your lying
that overwhelms me
but no longer believing you' . . .

Pause.

The attack is TODAY . . .
how can you not believe it . . .
and yet at the same time
why . . . why, then, believe it . . .

The Man with the Telephone
The attack is today . . . yes
very soon . . .
for sure RIGHT AWAY . . .
how else to BE LIVING
AS BELLIGERENTS . . .

Marie S.
We have all been condemned
to frivolousness and Empire . . .
Where did the story end . . .
Is there a story
a vital lead . . .
There is no story
for, to make a story
out of no story
that is not to partake of modernity . . .

The Second Witness
She doesn't want to admit it . . .
She wants now and for ever to forget it . . .
Still and all, in the sovereign cities
theatre is strictly forbidden
theatre is against the Law
against the democratic values of the Republic . . .
Theatre is a crime against Humanity
against the stars on the Flag
against the lordly rights of the Prince . . .

Marie S.
Reciting as if nothing had happened . . .
The storks . . . the storks . . .
And there we will see them wonder
faces veiled in media fright . . .
just enough of a little smile on their snouts . . .
Will she risk . . . will she go
so far as to unveil the root of her misfortune . . .
Would she dare ramble on just to lose us . . .
To tell ALL
as in the bloodiest tragedies . . .

She declaims.

> '*MADAME, JUSQU'ICI C'EST TROP TÔT*
> * M'ACCUSER .*
> *L'EMPEREUR N'A RIEN FAIT QU'ON NE PUISSE*
> * EXCUSER.*'
> 'IT IS TOO SOON, MADAM, ME THUS TO ACCUSE.
> THE EMPEROR HAS YET DONE NOTHING
> THAT CANNOT BE EXCUSED.'
> Even if my play wishes only to be
> a comedy without matter
> a tragedy meant for laughter . . .

The Man with the Telephone

> A whim for laughter . . .
> a BLOODTHIRSTY COMEDY . . .

Marie S.

> They panic
> facing a marble breast . . .
> not crossing off the roster of the dead . . .
> This is why they clamour for war . . .
> Our army
> is the Invincible Armada . . .
> To sustain
> the unthinkability of an error . . .
> No children amputated
> no women raped
> no prisoners sodomised
> no museums plundered
> a war of compassion
> a white CRUSADE . . .
> Justice's breast
> disseminates terror
> among the Highest
> Authorities of State . . .
> What then do we do
> when we are terrorised . . .
> We begin to hate
> all who resemble
> the mugshots, blacklisted features . . .

to hate those bushy beards
those eyes on fire
that troubling difference . . .

The Man with the Telephone
To HATE that difference
those beards on fire . . .

Marie S.
. . . besides, YOU
you are not unequivocally a man with a telephone
you are as troubling as they are . . .
YOU, you could most certainly be THEM . . .
Who might be in a position to reassure me
that you are not them . . .

The Man with the Telephone
Right . . . this is the point . . .
WHO could reassure me
that you are not them . . .

Marie S.
You have a cellphone . . .
that's how they proceed . . .
How many cellphones do you have . . .
you change them over and over . . .
I saw you take another one . . . yes
for it seems to me that we are
on MAXIMUM ALERT
even during the rehearsals
primarily during the rehearsals . . .

The Man with the Telephone
. . . on MAXIMUM ALERT . . .
during the rehearsals . . .
Didn't you say
it would be sacrilegious to . . .

Marie S.
My cross . . .
I don't have the RIGHT to get rid of it . . .
I carry my cellphone as one carries one's cross . . .

The cellphone is the CROSS . . .
Crucifixion of the human
the inhuman . . .
ECCE HOMO
ECCE FOEMINA
ECCE PARVULUS
You have many crosses
a ringing cross
a carillon cross
a war cross
perhaps even the swastika cross . . .
Wagner, Schubert, Beethoven . . .
announcing WAR, the ultimate HUBRIS . . .

The Man with the Telephone
I will not allow you to . . .
I have the right, do I not
not to be loved
not to seduce, not to look for trouble . . .

Marie S.
. . . the ultimate hubris, announcing
the APOCALYPSE . . .
The attack is planned for today
we must make haste to repeat
'See! . . . How she leans her cheek upon her hand
O that I were a glove upon that hand
that I might touch that cheek!'
To repeat, before
aphasia
apology
apostasy . . .
Defeat the policy of fear . . .
What does living mean
have you ever measured yourself
studiously, with determination
against such an unshirkable question . . .

The Man with the Telephone
To live . . .
to live . . . is . . . to let yourself live . . .

The Three Witnesses (*as if conversing among themselves*)
'Life – that is
continually shedding something that wants to die
Life – that is
being cruel and inexorable
against everything about us
that is growing old and weak
and not only about us
Life – that is, then
being without reverence for those who are dying
who are wretched, who are ancient
Constantly being a murderer
And yet old Moses said
Thou shalt not kill.'

Marie S.
Nietzsche or Moses . . . whom do you choose . . .

The Man with the Telephone
Being constantly a murderer . . .

He moves away.

Marie S.
Being constantly a machine of pleasure . . .
constantly the hand, the tongue
the thighs swift to
open Heaven wide . . .
Being constantly a liar
in expressing that bitter-sweet
truth of animal psyche . . .
despite the stupor in your eyes
from which every last glimmer of cognition
seems extinguished . . .

The Man with the Telephone (*leaving*)
You refer no doubt
to my inscrutable will
to perceive
to beef up my attention . . .

Marie S. (*running after him*)
   Would you too be afraid
   of my truths, alias my lies
   I have learned from them . . .
   They can infect you
   like Gospel truths . . .
   Mea culpa, mea maxima cul . . .
   What the Hell . . .
   might I be nothing
   but a secular catechism
   a republican missal . . .

The Third Witness
   She ventilated how in the cities
   with profaned cathedrals
   the ecclesiastical stars
   whispered voluptuously
   '*Sinite parvulos venire ad me*' . . .
   But Jesus said, according to Mark
   'And whosoever shall scandalise
   one of these little ones
   that believe in me
   it were better for him
   that a millstone were hanged
   around his neck
   and he were cast into the sea.'

Marie S.*'s cellphone rings, like an alert signal.*

Marie S.
   Hello . . . hello . . . hel . . . do vocalise something . . .
   Are you calling me in the shadows
   to announce nuclear catastrophes . . .
   You are THE imminence
   THE precipitation, THE ineluctable
   the overseer of the Apocalypse . . .
   Or else you are an avaricious heart
   at work practising
   shameful acts
   with the most enigmatic

attributes of yourself . . .
Could it be those very fingerings
condemned yesteryear
by some papal bull . . .
not everyone is granted
the sacrosanct right
to the wandering hand
that missal-white hand
scented with incense
mastering the martial art
of epidermic exploration
deftly poking
into pre-pubescent bodies . . .
Behind the grilles of confessionals
kneeling angels
have trespassed
the frontier of the prayer stool . . .
Hello . . . HELLO . . . do you know
that to remain silent
is to kill in the shadows . . .
I could catch you by the nose
as long as you had one
suitable for sniffing out danger
for all I know of you right now
is a panting breath
like a hunting dog . . .
Hello . . . hello . . .
Are you a dog . . .
Yes, you are a dog
bark, pleeease . . .
BARK . . .
Silence on the other end of the line . . .
Fool
there is no line
no cord
even no more the umbilical . . .
Only umbilici without port of registry
narcissistic mini-cyclops . . .
Hello . . . WHO are you . . .

What are you . . .
Non, non, pardonnez-moi
that's not what I meant . . .
I can hardly begin
by asking you
to give your personal particulars
even were you to be
less than a dog
not even if you had
different colour to my own
a political one I mean . . .
Hello . . . can you hear me
omit my question . . .
What is vital is not to succumb
to the insane temptation
to know everything in advance . . .
To act as if you were
the absolute stranger
unheimliche, the disturbing stranger
THE SELF, one of the first strangers . . .
STRANGER . . . I palpitate . . .
For you seem to solicit
an absolute listening
a maximal focus . . .
A prima donna . . .
And if you were Iago or Borgia or Lear . . .
Not Hamlet . . . no, not Hamlet
nor Don Juan . . .

The First Witness
Nor Orestes
Nor Coriolanus . . .
Nor George the First
Nor SoDoM the Last
Nor Talleyrand . . .

Marie S.
Besides, you remain too much
in the shadows
as if you had something else in mind . . .

In other words
in attending your resurrection . . .
This silence would seem to attest
that in your mouth
the earth is piling in
as if you had died to effort
died to hate . . .
Is this void of sound a precursor
to some . . . rummaging . . .
YOU . . . YOU . . .
my Primal Scream . . .
my Inquisitor . . .
my Persian Satrap . . .
my Fellow Creature . . .
See what abysses
have newly opened wide
their twilight eyes . . .

The Man with the Telephone (*offstage, in a dog-like voice*)
HEL O . . . my name is HEL O . . .
and you
do you know your name . . .
or else I am I
the only one here
who knows
what
you are called . . .

Marie S.
That is the point
I care little
for what I am called . . .

The Man with the Telephone (*offstage*)
I bet
you have mislaid your name . . .

Marie S.
MISLAID! . . . Indeed . . . *C'est bien cela* . . .
Perspicacity and Flair . . .

your talents however seem to be worn away
by a paronomastic industrial stain . . .
For you wish to apply pressure
do you not . . .
pressure
on the impressionability
which is the predicament of my gender . . .
The sphinx sloughing into a chameleon . . .
HELLO . . . hello . . . HEL O . . .

The Man with the Telephone
(*entering stage left, papers stuck to his shoes*)
I'd like to have a glance at these papers . . .
If you . . . *permettez,* I . . .

Marie S. (*looking at his feet*)
Neither sphinx nor chameleon
quite inevitably, a predator of this century . . .
You are on . . . an undisclosed training
let us say, rather . . . the winged messenger
of the One and Only Thinking . . .

The Man with the Telephone
This is a fucking unlaughing matter . . .
All the Agencies are on ALERT . . .
A theft of the highest gravity
has been committed . . .
Documents classified secret
have disappeared from the Archives
of the Highest Hall . . .
This disappearance might mean
the END OF THE WORLD . . .

Marie S.
The end of the world
now there's an exaggeration . . .
Even if I tell you
one must not exaggerate
I am already committing
a misdemeanour of exaggeration . . .

The Man with the Telephone
But this theft is a
satanic EXAGGERATION . . .
The question is this
how did they score
access to the Highest Hall . . .
how did they dare to profane
the limits of the world . . .
Isn't that
the pandemoniac exaggeration
of those fucking candidates
for the kilowatt throne . . .

Marie S.
You may find that
inconvenient, insolent
perhaps even hilarious
but they are terrorised
by Life
and Death
is their accomplice . . .
'When you are at home, you are dead'
Pascal already said, for he . . .

The Man with the Telephone
Fine . . . these dogs, then
should have stayed at home
if it was a question of
contempt for life . . .
It is out of the question for
our democratic values
to stop them
from dying at home
those rabid rats . . .
Out of the question, for us
to condemn
anyone whatsoever to live . . .

Marie S.
What a contemptuous leitmotiv

that QUESTION
questua du questeur
forgive me . . .
delighting in the quid pro quo
with the assiduousness of a cog . . .
In the end, all is imposture
how could we breathe without it . . .

The Man with the Telephone

Yeah . . . sure . . .
But I need now
to glance over these papers . . .
I need it, you understand . . .
It's a matter of an irrevocable need
absolutely unrepealable . . .

Marie S.

Comb, then, the papers
they are all over your shoes . . .
These documents are here
so that all may consult them
as need be, even, as you do, *pedibus calcantis* . . .

The Second Witness

You, the bibliolater
do you then not realize
that in the sterilised cities
they now create exclusively
books with blank pages . . .

Marie S.

At the crossing of the ways
an outdoor library
encyclopedia of misdemeanours
and masterpieces . . .
vertical labyrinth
for the ill-sighted
the hard of hearing
for claustrophobics
for illiterates . . .
'All symptoms

are a memory's distress'
We are all
called upon to brake
or to accelerate collapse
you too HEL O . . .
That is indeed your name, HEL O
which is a very odd name . . .
Might I be called Antigone or Phaedra
Clytemnestra or Colombina . . .
or else Madame Anti
the Stage Whore . . .

The Third Witness

You have foolishly broken the law . . .
You'd better learn this
in the democratic cities
it has been ruled that henceforth
it is forbidden to move about
without the three identity cards
established by the Constitution . . .
This crime, it goes without saying
is liable to the death penalty
in perpetuity . . .
TOLERANCE ZERO

Marie S.

Out of what primitive horde
have I fled . . .
what's this, this mist
this icy mist . . .
might a pain in the memory
be a question of meteorology . . .
In spite of all
ring out gusts of echoes
in my ear
and within my body
arise in archetypal stigmata
the familar and bloody branches
of your names . . .
Shame, shame, the last distress but one . . .

The First Witness

Alas . . . She knows not WHAT she knows . . .
And she thinks she knows WHAT she knows not . . .

The Man with the Telephone

Do you know these languages
these signs, these drawings . . .

Marie S.

. . . this cacography . . .
Am I here to give evidence
to certify that I have seen and heard . . .
or else to deny
deny everything . . .
NIHIL ABSOLUTO . . .

The Man with the Telephone

Mark my words . . .
denying everything
is always safer, denying
never confessing anything . . .
Besides being a courtesy of soul
it's an animal instinct . . .
Have foxes ever been seen
at confession . . .
what else is more trustworthy
than animality . . .
Ya, DENY
with aplomb, conviction
seduction, fucking charm . . .
to become both master and victim . . .
Deny . . . deny . . .
Negate, YA . . . no shame
but to me . . .
to ME alone
you must confess everything
TODO, got it
ALLES . . .

The Second Witness

In the vulture-cities

they say that to tell all
is the prettiest of deaths
the most graceful . . .

Marie S.

To tell all, *oui*
you are the irrefutable option . . .
the Inevitable Market
the Invisible Hand . . .
the State Man of God . . .
To tell you all
thanks to the brazen
irrepressible temptation
to institute before you
proceeding against myself . . .

The Third Witness

In the unrivalled cities
they talk of a plot hatched
against one's own class . . .
They talk above all
of a plot to Plot . . .
They talk of class, of hatching
and of Plot . . .
IF YOU'RE NOT WITH US
YOU'RE AGAINST US . . .

The Man with the Telephone

Then are you going
to lay these papers
these codes . . .
these coefficients . . .
these encodings . . .
these codicils . . .

Marie S.

As if you needed permission . . .
I no longer know . . .
Was my mission not
in times gone by
to lead the Pontifex maximus' rehearsals . . .

A matter of theatre, do you hear . . .
Have no fear
they will not notice a thing . . .
These papers are the spectacle
the population has been trained for . . .
it wished merely to satisfy
its appetite for frivolity and haemoglobin . . .
And then, from time immemorial
has not the spillage of blood
legitimised imperial pastimes
in the planet's Arenas . . .
Stop your worrying . . .
Rumours are abroad
that I withdrew these papers
to protect my family . . .
to cover up their offences
by hiding the secret of these files
during a public performance . . .

The Man with the Telephone

Funny . . . *WUNDERBAR*
clever . . . *grazioso* . . .
extraviadamente loco . . .
I have no personal opinion . . .
I am afraid, however, that
it would be a frame of mind
that they would hardly appreciate . . .
You are no doubt familiar
with their pusillanimous sense of humour . . .
the blood-steeped intransigence
of their CONSTIPATION . . .

Marie S.

An alarming dysfunction
for all satraps on duty . . .
but disarming
for a TYRANT OF DEMOCRACY . . .

The Man with the Telephone

But what got into your mind

what the hell got into YOU . . .
To do that . . .
not giving a fuck for your responsibilities
your function
your caste
your vassals
your celestial barber-queues . . .

The First Witness
In the hard-of-hearing cities
they foxtrot
to the sound of
soaring screech-vultures . . .

Marie S.
That's enough . . . it is impossible to foresee
a metamorphosis
before it takes place . . .
Am I here to confer
or to conjure . . .

The Man with the Telephone (*burrowing in the files, desperately*)
Too many . . . way too much
loads and loads . . . and goddam loads . . .
A paramount of toilet papers
bird-brain unfuckable texts . . .
A Tower of Babel of deadly documents
an avalanche of compromising snapshots
and this blood-soaked dust
which sticks to my hands
this slimy red dust . . .
I'll never manage . . .
You have to help me decipher
it's after all because of you
that I'm in this trap . . .
I have to decipher it all, ALL
before the others get here . . .
I only got a couple of seconds . . .
I've walked into a trap . . .

If you help me it's a trap . . .
If you agree to come with me
with or without papers, it's a trap . . .
If you remember your name
it's a trap . . .
TRAPPED . . .
I've even been caught in a trap
by telling you so . . .

The Second Witness

In the nuclear cities
the capital motto is
I AM TRULY THE GOOD . . .
Being myself justifies the lie
the spilt blood, the devastation
the carnages, the cruelty . . .
Being myself is to be infallible
flagrant, inevitable . . .
for Good is no other than Myself . . .

Marie S.

If I may make so bold
recollect yourself . . .
What then
the blood has newly deserted your cheeks
and your frantic eyes
search the sky that it may hold
the life escaping them . . .
These papers ARE the trap . . .
I did not encourage you
to walk into them . . .
I even warned you . . .
But you seemed to chastise me
for not owning
a Smith & Wesson
with which I might threaten you . . .
To reproach me for not being
one of those
Armed Females of America

one of those
Second Amendment Sisters . . .
Is yours not a . . . a . . .

The Third Witness

Contradictio in adjecto . . .

Marie S.

. . . A contradiction in terms . . .
To fight for PEACE
with a military arsenal
it's the latest chic
in the Empire World . . .

The First Witness

They are broadcasting
how in the fortified cities
the nuclear mini-bombs
used to usurp the hooligans
are out of stock . . .

The Man with the Telephone

You have forgotten the attack . . .
All of us will have forgotten it . . .
We are in a country where sparks are flying . . .

Marie S.

An attack . . .
What can we say to each other
when we are face to face . . .
One day I was told
'You have been branded like cattle . . . '
Do you see a mark on me
any mark whatsoever . . .

The Man with the Telephone (*approaching*)

Let's see . . .

He looks at the mountain of documents.

Do you have by any chance . . . a scar . . .
one of those disgusting
shrivelled and whitish things

keloidal perhaps
inflicted by surgeons
the most trendy on the planet
the very ones
whose manicured image
appears endlessly
on the cathode tube
as they plunge
their rubbery hands
into our open entrails
exposed to the camera . . .

He feels his belly.

. . . those flesh-tailors who love
to bray rejoicing
their questionable knowledge
the very ones
overprotected by Caesar
whom no one would dare
bring to Justice
for having cut
her healthy breast
or forgotten gauze pads
inside your apoplectic chest . . .
precisely those
who are so illiterate
they cannot tell
the difference
between a Heart of group A
and a Heart of group O . . .
double zero, heartless . . .

Pause.

. . . what the hell . . . what am I saying . . .
Forgetfulness got me . . .
absurd, unforgivable
this heart rising in my mouth . . .

Pause.

Forgive me . . .
I was saying . . .
do you have apex, an X
a Matrix . . . SORRY
a cicatrix
enfin, I mean
Marks . . .

The Second Witness

In the *emeritae* cities
every thrall
every threat
every three
every knee
every symptom
every axiom
every atom
must of necessity
bear its mark . . .

Marie S.

Come closer . . .

She opens her mouth.

Do you see
it's like the Queen Bee
a lazy queen . . .

The Man with the Telephone

Good heavens . . . a canine tooth
planted in the plane of the Palace . . .

Marie S.

Watch out
I am just as carnivorous
as an alphabet termite . . .

The Third Witness

In the narcissistic cities
'even their horses are carnivores' . . .

The Man with the Telephone

Once upon a time
I was only interested
in babes with greedy mouths
in ladies with forked tongues
in gluttonous females with glossy glottis . . .
But now
I have pinked in
to that Pink Palate . . . that Palace of Rose . . .
I have been dazzled
by this Promontory of Ivory . . .
I have been seized by this
breathtaking centripetal canine . . .

Marie S.

My lord, were I to succumb to your advances
how would you rid yourself of me . . .
You touch me . . . yes
there is no doubt that you touch me . . .
you kindle me, even . . .
Might you have arrived in these parts
with a proposal of nuptials . . .
Might we be allowed
to yield to the bowings of Love
to matrix a genital team
to care for nothing
but to mingle our loins
navigating from constellation
to constellation of castanets . . .

Pause.

Blind servitude
of the individual to the species . . .
We are on the high seas
and it seems to me that YOU
you cannot swim . . .
Do you know what a woman wants . . .
do you have the slightest id—

The Man with the Telephone
Marie S. . . . what do you really want . . .

Marie S.
Marie S.S.
my name . . . *horribile visu* . . .
horribile auditu . . .
Do you know that naming
is committing murder
TRAITOR . . .
Where do you come by
this fallacious information . . .
Marie, Mary, Mother of God
'Figlio, figlio, amoroso giglio' . . .
Immaculate Conception
as well as Virgin Conception . . .
too much honour . . .
SHE is the criminal . . .
she the deserter . . .
You blaspheme, sir . . .
Some have been struck
by lightning for less . . .
My identity, a configuration
a dance of atoms . . .
It may be you have
misunderstood the machine . . .
the papers you seek
may belong to other sarcophagi
they may have enrolled
in other *Constellations* . . .
Besides, do you have sufficient expertise
to crack this thorny problem . . .

The First Witness
In the digitalised cities
there might proliferate
nothing but specialists
whose scientific mission
consists in keeping

all thorny problems
wihout resolution . . .

The Man with the Telephone

It is cacodemonic to ask
such questions . . .
somehow, you seek to . . .
What do you really want, Marie S. . . .

Marie S. (*looking in the direction of a growing mechanical din*)

The brink of torture . . .
Setting the machines to sweat
as in olden times
setting the slaves to sweat . . .

The Man with the Telephone

I told you
you have to leave here . . .
These papers also
must be transferred from this place . . .
the borders must be padlocked
these documents kept safe
we must protect the cathode tube
the stadiums . . . the arenas . . .
and the oil . . . the oil . . .

Marie S.

. . . it was two and a half centuries ago
in the land of the Atridae . . .
Already then the citizens
had lost access
to the means of production . . .
Is it still licit
in this age of uproars
to be moved by such ineptitudes . . .

The Man with the Telephone

Halt . . . Leave that be . . .
There are no more antagonist functions . . .
all that is dead and buried
and the Earth won't stop spinning . . .

Marie S.
'IF CAIN SHALL BE AVENGED SEVENFOLD
TRULY LA'MECH SHALL BE AVENGED
SEVENTY AND SEVENFOLD . . . '
I will never return
to the HIGHEST HALL
NEVER AGAIN . . .

The Man with the Telephone
Goddammit to hell . . .
so what IS this fucking folly
which just plundered your mind . . .
What IS the night without lightning
wanting to gnaw at your days . . .
No one leaves the HEIL-HALL . . .
Do you believe in freedom . . .
This is an instantly unpatriotic
provocation . . .
A provocation more murderous
than a rocket launcher . . .
An impossible atomic dice thrown
on the table of the Untouchables . . .

He goes up to her.

What DO you really want
Marie S. . . .

The Third Witness
In the gargantuan cities
the sole constitutional desire
is the obese desire
to desire eternally . . .
DESIRE is the LAW
for there is no Law without Desire . . .

Marie S.
Chastising me in such fashion . . .
Stranger, watch out . . .
today the more we know
the more our sphere of activity

becomes exiguous . . .
Straniero . . . Unheimliche
my shadowy eyes
infer that I know you . . .
but all the same
a dyspeptic contradiction
which seems to be your essence
the twitch which suits you
to stifle the ready step
your geometric doubts
your technological silences
seems obstinately
to shy away from my memory . . .
Stranger
why then
this unlearned knowledge
this neuronal faltering
where YESTERDAY
has bolted up its archives . . .

The Man with the Telephone
Fuck the past, fuck the memory . . .
for you it is today that counts . . .
you must accept, you must bend . . .
strike down the error and not the errant . . .

Marie S.
Your Excellency the Errant
you seem to know
where your fucking steps are leading you . . .

The Man with the Telephone
It's true, I am the universal . . .
you are only the particular . . .
I am a brain . . . a compass
and not a flunkey . . .
A man with grey matter
nowadays
is a priceless commodity . . .

Marie S.
The deuce! . . . You back-alley gutless dunghill-cock . . .

The Man with the Telephone
A woman
should not surrender to
this military jargon . . .
A woman should not . . .

Marie S.
Nor raise her voice . . .
Nor uncross her legs . . .
Nor run for President . . .
Nor approach a rent boy in a red-light district . . .
Nor claim the same salary as males . . .
Nor become a cardinal or a rabbi, or an ayatollah
Nor spit . . . Nor grow old . . .
Nor discourse upon Philosophy . . .
Nor sexually harass
economically dependent young men . . .

The Man with the Telephone
A woman is a woman
and will always remain a woman . . .
There's nothing you can do about it
that's clear enough . . .

Marie S.
Siding with an antiphrastic choice . . .
as clarity goes, that is clearly unclear . . .
Then tell me
what is a father . . .

The Man with the Telephone
Christ . . . why me . . .
why ask just me this indelicate question . . .
A father is nothing but a Father . . .

The Three Witnesses
'He used to say,
Do His will as if it were thy will,
that He may do thy will as if it were His will

Annul thy will before His will
that He may annul the will of others
before thy will' . . .
So it is written
in the *Mishna II* of the *Treatise of the Fathers of the world* . . .

Marie S.
And what if the father were a dog . . .

The Man with the Telephone
A dog is a dog . . .
But a woman
what's more heart-shaking . . .

Marie S.
The real heart-shaking
would be to fight . . .

The Man with the Telephone
Fight . . .
A moth-eaten plan
they're bringing back to life . . .

The Three Witnesses
'Die Gewalt ist Geschichtehebamme' . . .
Violence is the midwife of History . . .

The Man with the Telephone
As for myself, I left the army
I sat tight
maybe in the Vatican . . .
or possibly in Texas . . .
But you . . . you . . .

Marie S.
A deserter . . . a trotter . . .
and not a conscientious objector . . .
What were you doing in the Texas-Vatican . . .
Did you take part in Rodeo Conclaves . . .
did you wear a purple cassock
and pointed boots with spurs . . .
did you arrogantly administer

presidential blessings
Your Holiness, the apostate . . .

Down on one knee, she kisses his hand.

The Man with the Telephone
Wait . . .
I seem to hear
suspicious sounds . . .
The attack . . . we almost forgot the attack . . .

Marie S.
The attack
spurred on by the chuckling
of children . . .

The Man with the Telephone
Children . . .
do you mean, *hyena ridens*
laughing hyenas . . .
I'll go and take a look all the same . . .
Haven't you got
a defence weapon
a Kalashnikov
a Rocket Launcher
a truncheon, a cudgel . . .

Marie S.
Children seem
to have a paroxysmal effect
on your production of adrenalin
far more than the *Éminences Grises*
of State Crime . . .
Despicable old chiseller
afraid of
baby Red Riding Hood . . .
Jealousy is ruining you . . .
character IS destiny . . .
These little creatures
let them get oxygen . . .

they are the only ones
who still know
how to play at war
without saddening us
at the pitiful spectacle
of their poverty-stricken attributes
in an indigent semi-erection . . .

The Man with the Telephone
Children . . .
There are only rats left . . .
Wait, don't move . . .
I'll flush you out those mujahidin . . .

*He takes his shoe in his hand and a round of rifle bullets out of his
pocket . . .*

*A moment later he comes back with two children: a little boy, whom he
is pulling by the ear, and a little girl, whom he drags by the hand.*

Marie S.
Power . . . the sly seizure of power
gripped by the imparity in level
between two paces . . .
You, Herod
the Presbyterian brain
dragging in that manner
two innocent souls, are you not . . .

The Man with the Telephone
. . . two cherubic souls devoting themselves
to the theft of State documents
to filching uniforms from the elite troops
of our Holy Nation . . .

Marie S.
Theatre paraphernalia . . .
tin crowns . . .
Theatre . . .
they love theatre . . .
el teatro del mundo . . .

The Man with the Telephone
It makes you sick to your stomach to see that
beat the hell out of you
snotty-nosed . . .
But for Christ's sake
what the hell are your parents up to . . .

Little Girl (*mischievously*)
They're catchin' z's . . .

Marie S.
Z's . . . Zeus! . . . what does she mean
by this blasphemous code . . .
Might their parents be at prayer . . .
The otium . . . The opium of the people . . .
Are the leftist neighbourhoods
as pious as that . . .
can they be, like cowards
boycotting the strike . . .

Little Boy
Word . . .
in the 'hood
only the kids get up in the mornin' . . .

The Man with the Telephone
Fine education . . .

Marie S.
How odd all of this . . .
Why then do you rise
at sunrise . . .

Little Boy
She buggin' or what
to go to school . . . feel me . . .

The Man with the Telephone
While the parents are asleep . . .
Bunch of lazy good-for-nothings . . .
The USA, master of the world
and these morons spend their lives
like Sleeping Beauties . . .

Little Boy

The whole 'hood's assed out . . .
I mean, *über*-out-of-job
'cause a shady address is a misdemeanour
a dirty mug is a ugly crime . . .

Little Girl

Zero misdemeanours for my teach'
the alphabet-slinger
on maternity leave . . .
she's got sixty-two candles
and's knocked up with three seeds . . .

The Man with the Telephone

And you're cutting class
using your sticky fingers
to raid the rest area . . .

Little Boy

Who're you kiddin' . . .
for us, rest is dead, stiff, cold . . .
down to the burial ground
86'ed to the wooden kimono . . .
So you can stick your sticky fingers
you know where . . .
Hella better than rusting away with the rotten bars
at the foot of the projects . . .
WE be the freebie soldiers . . .
The old signora say
you hafta BE free on your own
so, we ain't gonna drop the ball . . .
Man
we ain't finna live like oreos neither . . .
chewin' our brains out for this . . .
Knahmean? . . .

Marie S.

An actor
a born performer . . .
what verve, what substance . . .
More pathos than Olivier

more electric intensity than Brando . . .
more magnetism than Marlene . . .
PEREJEVANIE, PEREJEVANIE . . .
And what is more, a gifted tragedian . . .
Pity and Terror . . .
Did you not notice . . .
he has mastered the System wonderfully
he plays moment by moment
he opens his face to the audience
he plays on distanciation
he rises in immobility
he creates the Brechtian *gestus*
he has understood all of it
I believe you, I believe you, my boy . . .

Pause.

. . . however, young man
please forgive me . . .
your genitor
your father, that is
what does he say . . .

Little Boy
Crazy
yo lady, you lookin' to catch you
some cheap thrills . . .
The dead beat ain't got nuthin' to say . . .
Feel me? . . .

Little Girl
Stop frontin' . . .
he say soon
he gonna get a gig . . .
he gonna . . .

Little Boy
Shut yo face, lil' pigeon . . .

Little Girl
He say soon
he'll be stackin' dead presidents

and heads'll be rollin' off
Capitol Hill . . .

Little Boy
Yeah, dream on . . .

Little Girl
Yo, s'up with breakin' us off
with a lil' ice . . .
a Benji . . . some big faces . . .
a Roman sesterce . . .
like, some chi-ching, bling, cream, bones, ends . . .

Marie S. (*slaps her*)
Thou . . . my dear, I mean
you should
never forget
that you belong
not only
to the human species
but, in addition
and which is essential
to the female gender
my *damoiselle* . . .
Never forget
that it is better to steal
than to ask for charity . . .

Little Boy
Screw your kind
hoochy-hooch . . .
C'mon, shorty . . .
this chick is wack
she ain't got nuthin' for us, anyway . . .

They leave. The **Little Boy** *sings and dances to hip-hop.*

Marie S. (*running after them*)
Children
you have all my
republican consideration
not because of your

personal data
I mean to say
your diminutive age . . . no . . .
but because you seem to be
spurred by other determinations
moved by other designs
and I do mean DISEGNI
than those of . . . of . . .
resignation addicts . . .
your pusillanimous
deathly genitors . . .

Little Girl (*in the distance*)
A genital – whassat
whassa deadly pussy-ominous . . .

Little Boy
It's when you a old ho
like her . . .

The **Little Girl** *and the* **Little Boy** *vanish.*

The Man with the Telephone
You seem to have lost
your flair for strategy, Madame . . .
Since when do you allow
some joker
to spray you with spit . . .
Where did you unearth
that crown of thorns . . .
The Che Nazarene
is a dated icon . . .
What's crucial is staying alive
it only takes
letting yourself go . . .
What is the point of involving these . . .
these . . . neighbourhood rejects
these micro-copies of Talibans . . .

Marie S.
I felt that blow in my own flesh . . .

The Man with the Telephone (*violently, scornfully*)
All you did was hit a runt
a starveling from the wrong side of the beltway
a paltry thing, a defeatist . . .

The Three Witnesses
HAAAAAAAIUUUUUUH
TRRRRRRTRRRRRTRBRR . . .

Noises of fighter planes.

Marie S.
Wrath . . .
Olympian war games . . .
turning all men
back into clay . . .
chess game
between colossi and pygmies . . .
destroying
the library of King Ashurbanipal
with its three thousand tablets . . .
being deaf, deaf
utterly deaf . . .
Opening the place where Zeus
locked up the Titans . . .
Speaking to them in Aramaic
the language of Christ . . .
Alas, I owe them my obedience
obedience of the soil
obedience of the blood . . .
I am like them
steeped in the same griefs
the same crimes . . .
I have shared
moons and suns with them . . .
have I not trod with them
the path between the scarlet columns
that has led us to here . . .

The Man with the Telephone
Time is slipping away from us

Marie S. . . .
Is your heart still set
on turning down my request . . .
I need help . . .
It is known
that a man
is biologically inferior . . .
Isn't it because of you
that I'm in this place . . .
I have to decipher the whole
decode everything . . .
a labour of Titan . . .
to recover
who knows what keys
buried in the mountain . . .
to lead the alabaster bull
to the source of the river . . .
I have to compel you
by incitation
beg you by force
to give me back
the secret weapon
the Torah, the Koran, the Bible
the password
of the Thematocracy . . .
because the attack
you do understand
the ATTACK is imminent . . .

As if in a trance:

. . . Soon we will see horses
screaming in the flames . . .
THIS is the wrath of the Excellencies
setting fire to the mountain's limbs . . .
this is the Amphitheatre of the world
with a masonry of refugees' flesh . . .

He blows his nose.

And I, I am becoming incapable
of detecting in the crowd
the chemical odour of the enemy . . .

Marie S.

Where have our nano-machines of war
gone to hide
machines for scenting danger
gravedigger-robots
mechanical half-breed hounds . . .
Why then this distress . . .
your spirits should be high . . .
do you not sit
at the side of their throne
at the side of the one
who rules only by Decree . . .

The Man with the Telephone (*trembling*)

The Decree . . . of course . . . that digital trash . . .
THE DECREE . . . they rule only by decree . . .

As if to himself:

What the Hell . . .
'You will no longer fear
when you no longer hope' . . .

Marie S.

Where is this coming from
so unprompted, so inopportune
so overwhelming
this licentious lust
to copulate with you . . .

The Man with the Telephone

Seneca, you see . . .
a memory of bygone years . . .
Youth did one day have to fade . . .
I must have
been afflicted too
with the Mephistophelian vice

of burrowing in books . . .
the length of a sickness
of an itch, of an engine failure . . .
In my intoxication
I happened to dream sometimes
to DREAM, you understand . . .
I dreamed of violent seismic shocks . . .
of a . . . of a . . .
violent commotion
of the political order . . .
I dreamed of . . . of revolutionising
the world market . . .
a heresiarch, you understand . . .
It's absurd, isn't it
Childish . . .
an outlaw, who dreamed of writing
what it is not permitted to read . . .
It was like a curse
an alcoholism of the soul
a Maoism of the blood
a diarrhoea of the mind . . .
But I got over it very quickly . . .
thanks to prayer . . .
I was a hair away from entering
the Presbyterian Orders . . .
I was not made for deciphering
for command . . .
It is true that I was wrong
and they were right . . .
I like to be given orders . . .
I feel a genuine joy
in carrying them out . . .
I never argue with them
I never ask
the slightest question
about just how exact they are
or just how JUST, either . . .
Each man has his calling . . .
an order is an order

it's not my place
to judge it, even less
to argue with it . . .
And how fatiguing, how worrying
if I had to submit after that . . .
that's MY freedom . . .
I'm an executor
we also have indeed
our importance . . .
without us, nothing would be done
the world could not keep turning
if we were all commanders . . .
I know I am only a cog
in a mechanism I do not understand
and I'm happy like that . . .
I'm happy, Marie S. . . .

Marie S.
Come here . . . come closer . . .
what would you say
to being reconciled
with . . . the female gender
the fair sex . . . *le sexe second* . . .

She approaches, attempts to fondle him.

The Man with the Telephone
I'm lukewarm
moderately autistic
essentially circumspect . . .

Marie S. (*coming up very close to him*)
. . . wait . . .
you are beginning to have
eyes like a pit bull
a Majorcan mongrel
an Argentine mastiff
a bad boys' dog
the kind that are
known unfavourably
to law enforcement patrols . . .

The Man with the Telephone
You make me happy . . .

Marie S.
Break with the past . . .
embrace the keen art of the instant . . .
that is what sexual is . . .

The Man with the Telephone
. . . the sexual, yes . . . the tomb . . .

Pause.

Shh . . . LISTEN . . . wait . . .
I hear suspicious noises . . .

Marie S.
The children coming back . . .

She smiles sarcastically.

They armed the children . . .

The Man with the Telephone
Children too
can be monsters
tyrants . . .

Marie S.
You, my child
you could be my father . . .

The Man with the Telephone
Shh . . . Listen . . .
I'd better leave . . .
Do you understand . . .
I have to go . . .
CARTAGO DELENDA EST . . .

He runs off into the mountain.

Marie S.
Let the Mountain of Writings
be brought
to the theatre . . .

Let the children make haste
if their appetite for play
has not flown with their youth . . .

The Three Witnesses
In the cities spreadeagled by kicks
from 'the colossus straddling the world'
the children say with Seneca
'Though I despise my life, I am master of yours' . . .

The Two Children (*entering, at the back of the auditorium*)
That's what's up, let's motivate
keep it rollin' . . .
Crossin' the highway
sure is better 'n rottin' away
in the rusted-out projects . . .

Blackout.

Midnight strikes on a vast theatre stage . . .

There are obvious signs of violent events . . .

The Little Girl *and* **The Little Boy** *emerge from the prompter's box.*

Little Girl
Jerks . . . they really did cut outta here . . .

Little Boy
This is shitsville . . .
these goddam ballbusters
should be locked up . . .

Little Girl
That's what's up . . .
We're stuck . . .
This place is offta meter-spooky . . .
At midnight
cities got no more watchdogs . . .

Pause.

> Don't hafta tell ya, if we hadn't a hid
> we'd a got our faces smashed in . . .
> we'd be totally slammed
> iced-ovah, checked out . . .

Little Boy

> Go get Alcatrazzed . . .
> Who in their right mind had the libido to stay here
> and me like some dipstick listenin' to you . . .
> How'm I gonna figure
> what I can't get my head round . . .
> Say, even a two-bit bandit knows
> it's the one that guards you kills you . . .

Little Girl

> Sparks were flyin' out the frame
> the whole joint was explosive . . .

Little Boy

> They were just after the creepy hag . . .
> Anyhow I don't like her grill . . .

Little Girl

> What's up with her features
> take a look at your own . . .
> And what about the others
> with their pit-bull muzzles
> like them better . . .

Little Boy

> Strap your muzzle on . . .
> Shit, it's *über*-goth here
> Don't like that . . .
> It's not my thing
> hangin' in dead corners . . .
> Like that's all there was to do
> grindin' in sufferin' and blood . . .

He takes out a paper and reads.

'Basically we expect
very original solutions
from very conformist minds
is this the best means
of filling in the gaps
and of healing the cracks' . . .
That's it, cracked, they're all cracked . . .
for real . . .
so, you have some kinda solution
yeah, you, you . . . very conformist mind
to get us outta this shitsville . . .
It's dead, I'm tellin' ya . . .
Wait . . . wait lemme see . . .
this . . . shit's bangin'
hey, man . . .
wouldja listen to their bull about Aids . . .

He reads.

'It alters our love relationships
at the very root' . . .

Little Girl

. . . Yeah . . . no question . . .
if you love me
start by suspectin' me . . .

Little Boy

We're standin' in shit
for real, I'm tellin ya . . .
you can't even get
easy puss no more . . .
If you don't watch out
we're goin' crash and burn . . .
you can catch the HIV and die
suckin' on your mama's tit . . .

Little Girl

It ain't like that
you lil' son of a bourge—
You can't even

rub somebody up
without gettin' scared you'll die . . .

Little Boy

Shorty, you bustin' my b . . .
Gives you a hard-on, huh
to know I'm playing the sidelines . . .

Little Girl

That's a given . . .
if you've got it, you're all infected
sweat an' even tears . . .

Little Boy

No question . . . I get it . . . I fill you . . .
But just try cryin' round me
and I'll shower you in the purest . . . Clorox . . .

Little Girl

Chill . . . it'd . . . be cooler'n fat L . . .

Little Boy

No, gonna be the death of
the booboo buddies . . .

Little Girl

Better believe it . . . same nerve as the old man . . .
I always said it
rather be a bastard than my father's daughter . . .

Pause.

Waaaow . . . I'm buggin', I'm seein' things . . . Listen
to this . . .

She reads.

'Each man present in this room
is merely half the man
his grandfather was' . . .
So you
you'd just be
a quarter of your gran'pappy . . .

Little Boy (*trying to pull the paper away from her*)
>You gonna stop with your parlayin'
>or I'll bust you in the grill . . .
>when you're the . . . lumpen prolo—

Little Girl
>Yo, man, calm down . . .
>The wangstas strong-arming the staircase
>don't impress me no more . . .
>Wait . . . you're gonna like this . . .

She reads.

>'At fourteen years of age the average American
>will have seen 11,000 murders on TV' . . .

Little Boy
>Ain't we lucky . . .
>Great welcome
>from Mama Liberty . . .

Little Girl
>Yeah, that's fresh, dope . . .
>soul-steering, spine-tingling . . .

Little Boy
>Shit . . .
>what the hell are we doin'
>in this fucked-up theatre . . .
>Like we got nuthin' better to bag . . .

Little Girl
>Straight, I hear ya . . .
>but spendin' your life playin'
>is not as scary as playin' with your life . . .

Little Boy
>Shut up . . . They're comin' back, for sure . . .

Little Girl
>Sure they ain't . . .
>didn't you get it
>they were in a hurry

to get the hell outta here
with their skitzin' machines
and her whatsitmeans . . .
Didn't you see them goin'
surgery-crazy to rip them off her . . .
Didn't you hear her screamin'
and then the rag in her mouth
full of toilet water . . .
and the blood spatterin' . . . the blood . . .
And the audience that couldn't stop clappin' . . .
Morons . . . they thought it was *Pulp Fiction* . . .

Little Boy

Get outta here . . . whose fault is it . . .
I ain't the one wanted
to get up on the stage . . .
I ain't the one wanted
this . . . entertainment massacre . . .
I ain't the one . . .

Little Girl

Oh, that's great . . .
Brando, that wasn't you, huh . . .
and Che, that wasn't you . . .
you even started spoutin'
in Bolivian, chewin' your words
like Marlon on the *Waterfront* . . .
Wasn't it you said yes first . . .
you couldn't stop jokin'
you cast me down like Cassandra
you couldn't stop flossin' that flow . . .
But them . . .
they didn't look like they were jokin' . . .
they never joked . . .
Their eyes
were the spit of Cain's eyes . . .

Pause.

One helluva a job this . . .
Still . . .

maybe it's true that here
we'd actually be allowed to act . . .

Little Boy
And why not
ridin' a Ferrari with the top down, chrome spinnin' . . .
you can keep on fantasizin' . . .
we're up shitscreek, I'm tellin' you . . . ain't gonna last . . .
You looked at us, huh . . .
Who do you think you are, Dr Rice . . .
huh . . . you wouldn't be lookin'
like that ho Condi by any chance would ya . . .

Little Girl
And you
you're the spit of the Chief Commander
all g'd up like a fighter pilot . . .

Little Boy
What . . . don't sweat it
soon as we lay our hands on their toilet paper
they're gonna liquidate us . . . peace . . .
Round here they don't need no lil' youths from the zone
no slimy scum like us two . . .

Little Girl
Slimy, yourself . . .
Assholes . . . fightin'
butcherin' each other for paper trash
for Chupa-Chup papers . . .

Little Boy
That's it . . . how you figure . . .
maybe it's acid
moolah
oil they're lookin' for . . .
weapons of mass terror . . .

Little Girl
And all that in a fuckin' theatre . . .
It's like if you said we were orderin'
caviar n' champagne in the ghetto . . .

Little Boy

What if it was a Resolution
they were lookin' for . . .
a War Permit, huh . . .

Little Girl

Like . . . why not the letter
lil' Jesus wrote
his mama . . .

Little Boy

Quit tryin' . . . I ain't gonna think you're funny . . .
But your Mary-Spy though
she was pretty mashed up . . .

Little Girl

She slipped me this writing . . .
And another one . . .
Damn, they've got bloodstains on them . . .
it's disgustin' . . .
They beat her on the head . . .
it's disgustin' . . .
She looked at me
like she was sayin'
I had to learn this thing by heart . . .
If you want I can read it to you . . .

Little Boy

Now you got me laughin' . . .
You blown a fuse or what . . .

Little Girl

Listen, listen to this

She recites:

'Men are not my fellow creatures
they are those who look at me and judge
my fellows are those who love me
and who do not look at me
who love me in spite of all
who love me against degeneracy
against baseness

against betrayal
myself and not what I have done or will do
who love me as I would love myself' . . .

Little Boy

She's wall-to-wall wasted . . .
You catch a word
out of that stuff . . .

Little Girl

That stuff, excuse you me, is . . .
Malraux's *The Human Condition* . . .

Little Boy

Say what . . .
The Woman Cont . . . diction . . .

Little Girl

Stopiiiiit . . . ignoramus . . .
The Human Condition . . .
by the French Head of Culture
from last century . . .
the dude, dig . . .
who decided to shampoo
the buildings in Paris . . .

Little Boy

And our
pigsty housing projects
got no right
to a cultural shampoo . . .
Who cares . . .
Let them regurgitate . . .
illiterate puke . . .
Fuckin' shit
I'll give them some
of that CULTURE I got up my ass . . .

Little Girl

Your butt
'll always be
your favourite whippin' boy . . .

Little Boy

>Sure . . .
>you look at the US of A . . .
>are they gonna fuckin' bother
>with a Secretary for Culture . . .
>ain't had enough in the homeland . . .
>It's hell here . . . like
>only Secretaries for War
>and . . . that's it . . .
>Need to get our rocks off on somethin' . . .

Little Girl

>You . . . you're just a
>willin' slave . . .
>stripped naked, consentin'
>and clappin' your hands . . .
>You change your mind
>more often than your diapers . . .
>you got no style, you know . . .
>you went out with the twist . . .

Little Boy

>Peep this chick . . .
>willin' slave . . . stripped naked and cunt-scentin' . . .
>how old are you huh . . .
>she still believes in Mama Santa Klaus . . .
>as if they left us the choice . . .
>Anyway, don't knock yourself out
>it doesn't even turn me on
>your intelligent way
>of bein' stupid . . .
>and just quit crampin' my style like that
>OK . . .

Pause.

Little Girl

>And now
>what we gonna do . . .
>we freezin' our brain juice here . . . I'm cold . . .

I'm wiped, I'm beat
I am goin' dead from thirst . . .

Little Boy

And me, man I'm dyin' from starvation . . .
You wouldn't happen to be hidin'
a big strawberry sundae
with cherries up the ass
and some real gunky chocolate on top . . .
A big dessert from a waffle-diner, huh . . .

Little Girl

Sir, yes, sir . . .
Right there I saw . . . there . . . under the trash
a ham 'n mustard roll
bodega-style
just the thing for a big gangsta like you . . .

She brings it to him.

Little Boy

Shit, squashed like a rat . . .
Ain't you got somethin' else not so . . . sushi . . .

Little Girl

Yeah . . . better believe it
somethin' sexy
juicy, soft
the greatest, right . . .
Oh no, whaddya know . . .
burned, screwed . . .
hafta be superhuman to lay your hands on that . . .

Little Boy

On what . . .

Little Girl

The latest weapon of the USA . . .

Little Boy

Toootally . . .
the atomic mini-suitcase . . .

Little Girl

Negative . . .

Little Boy

The GBU 28
the precision-guided bomb, 4,400 pounds . . .
the hyper-humane weapon, right . . .

Little Girl

Cosmo-negative . . . mega-nuthin' . . .
I'm talkin 'bout the fearsome weapon
the real one
the one you can mistreat all you want
capable of withstanding
parachute-landing shocks
climatic temperatures from hell
the truly indestructible weapon . . .
You followin' me . . .

Little Boy

Nanotech . . .
Hypersonic drones . . .

Little Girl

Don't get scientific on me . . .

Little Boy

Go ahead . . . spit it out . . .

Little Girl

The new generation sandwich . . .
the pocket sandwich . . .

Little Boy

Gotta lay off the acid . . .

Little Girl

No, I ain't foolin' . . . live and direct . . .
It can stay fresh for three years
at 79 degrees . . .
but in the Gulf, ain't so lucky
at 100 degrees, you can only keep it eatable
six lousy months . . .

Little Boy
Sounds real pukey
your futuristic cookin' . . .

Pause.

. . . But your . . . inorganic stuff
got me salivatin' . . .

Little Girl
Dismissed . . .
only got rat-ham-mustard
on the menu . . .

Little Boy
Gimme it then . . .
Say, rats are more . . . biological
than your pocket garbage . . .

Pause.

Little Girl
I'm on to it . . . It's starin' me in the face . . .

Little Boy
You've still got a bone to chew . . .

Little Girl
They shut us up in here
to coerce us to search . . .

Little Boy
Yeah sure . . .
co-search for rats . . .

Little Girl
To search for what they're searchin' for . . .
They're usin' us . . .
they played us for suckers again . . .

Little Boy
Hey . . . are you picturin' you're
one of the *Little Bees* from Colombia . . .
one of the Sri Lanka *Baby Brigade* . . .

Little Girl

The kids who're forced to beat
and kill their kin
even to EAT them . . .

Little Boy

OK . . . creepy scene . . .
Fat chance with the food . . .
too bad we're not in Sierra Leone . . .

Little Girl

Ain't you ashamed to laugh at those kids . . .

Little Boy

At least THEY're not obliged
to meet death all mutilated . . .

Little Girl

What's the difference . . .

Little Boy

They inject them
with crack
to stop them bawlin' . . .
to make them courageous . . .

Little Girl

Courageous . . .
to amputate people
kill them
cook them
and eat them . . .

Little Boy

I'm flippin' the channel . . . Little pussy de Sade . . .
you askin' for a whippin' . . .

Pause.

. . . anyhow, now
I need one of their jambaa blunts
illico presto . . .

Little Girl

    You scared, you are . . .
    I've got
    a jackhammer in my belly too . . .
    those guys ain't kiddin'
    with their three-piece suits, an' all that . . .
    say peace to your gangsta patch on the stoop . . .
    they've talked clear-cut
    an' with every mama's son . . .

Pause.

Little Boy

    We have to start searchin' . . .
    We're child soldiers . . .
    We have to tote weapons . . .
    They want us to kill
    to drink blood
    and before the battle
    to undergo
    an incision in the temple
    next to the right eye . . .
    and to let them inject us
    with cocaine . . .

Little Girl

    We are child soldiers . . .
    Us girls
    if we won't give them sex
    they're gonna shoot us
    in the vagina . . .
    They enjoy
    opening the bellies of our pregnant sisters
    to win bets about the sex of the foetus . . .

Little Boy

    'I got signed up
    during operation *Knock Over* . . .
    I was nine years old . . .
    They came through the backyard . . .

"We want to take a child like you
with us . . . we like you" . . .
My mother doesn't say a word . . .
she stifles a scream . . .
My father reacts . . .
they threaten to kill him . . .
They yell at him behind the house . . .
I heard a gunshot
One of them said to me
"Let's go, they killed your father" . . .
One of their women
grabbed me by the hand brutally . . .
She dragged me with her . . .
When we passed
behind the house
I saw the eyes of my dead father' . . .

Little Girl

'My fellow soldiers
were between eight and thirteen years old . . .
They all had war-nicknames . . .
Fist had not found
a single member of his family left alive . . .
Stabb prayed God to forgive him . . .
Tiger had the motto of his brigade
incised in capital letters in his chest . . .
Hike had been forced several times
to cut off the right hand of civilians
and to slap them bloody with it' . . .

Little Boy

'I was
a boy commander . . .
I commanded ten children
between ten and sixteen years old . . .
I remember
when I was handling
the big machine gun
nobody dared to step in front of me . . .

You, move and I'll shoot you down, I used to say . . .
I felt strong and powerful . . .
I wasn't scared of anythin' . . .
I gave no value
to any human feeling' . . .

Little Girl *and* **Little Boy**
We are child soldiers . . .
we have to tote weapons . . .
we have to drink blood . . .
we are ferocious . . .
around our necks we wear
our cyanide capsules . . .
we are child soldiers . . .

The Three Witnesses (*marching in, singing like an army chorus*)
If you've fallen on the ground
it's the fault of the bounds
with your nose in the gutter
it's the fault of the rotter . . .

Little Girl (*to* **The Three Witnesses**)
OK, the fun and games are over . . .
where has the God
of Armies got to . . .

The First Witness
Ma'am, yes, ma'am . . .

The Second Witness
Sir, yes, sir . . .

The Third Witness
Ma'am, yes, sir . . .
Sir, yes, ma'am . . .

The Man with the Telephone (*running in from the orchestra*)
They are saying by the thousands
'Pre-emptive war
is war of aggression'
do you understand . . .
of AGGRESSION . . .

Little Boy
Hey you listen . . .
have you kinda forgotten
that they had the guts
to look us in the iris . . .
so didn't you get that they wanted
to make tartar with our imperial balls . . .

The Three Witnesses (*overlapping*)
Sir, yes, sir . . .

Little Girl
PEACE, the poor fool . . .
she was stayin outta trouble
she wasn't botherin bubble
but those paranoid petty king-manimals
sent the damn Peace to the hospital . . .

The Three Witnesses
Ma'am, yes, ma'am . . .

The Man with the Telephone (*still running*)
They're rumbling all around
'War of aggression
violates the international
humanitarian law
to which all nations are bound to' . . .

Little Girl (*to the* **Little Boy**)
So did you finally do the math . . .
There is no point
in spittin' out your lungs . . .

She mocks him.

'War of aggression
violates the international
humanitarian law
which all nations
are bound to respect' . . .
RESPECT . . . my ass . . .

The Man with the Telephone *runs offstage.*

Little Boy
Ma'am, fuck, ma'am . . .

Pause.

So you finally found the toilet paper
they wanted to bomb . . .

Pause.

Sounds of explosions mingle with the screams of **The Little Girl**,
The Little Boy *and* **The Three Witnesses**, *who rush offstage
while* **Marie S.** *is heard crying out 'CROSS . . . DISASTER . . .
DISTRESS . . . MOURNING . . . '*

Marie S. *enters the wrecked stage, her head bandaged, under a rain of
sand.*

Marie S.
Cross . . . disaster . . . distress . . . mourning . . .

Pause.

Quirites, my fellow citizens, alas
why and wherefore
this incomparable lightness
beyond matter
beyond irrepressible whims
groans gurgling with blood
clashes of Empire . . .
An eternity has henceforth
gone by
between before
and now . . .
NUNC ET HODIE . . .
The world is deserted . . .
the void seems challenged only
by the suffocating weight
of goods in transit . . .
the studious promenades
of contaminated ruminants

butchered swine
poisoned water
schizoid veal's heads
lethal sponges
destined for
the summer camps . . .
And that malediction
man-eating viruses
a croaked anthem
to the terrestrial condition
which loves to wallow
in the triumvirate
of gold
of the gymnasium
of the martial parade . . .
That is the life we love . . .
Are we villains by necessity . . .
We will be judged . . .
Joyous animals in the cosmic microwave
background radiation . . .
At what point in the day
did we succeed . . .
The evening opens resplendent . . .
the sun will doubtless
set the horizon on fire
in blood-soaked nuptials . . .
All seems becalmed . . .
the children too have gone . . .
which of them
has taken
our belongings purloined fromThanatos . . .
What are they looking for
in the tininess
of the female dust
on these tablets of clay . . .
I pretended to know . . .
Tantalos-Knowledge
repeating *ab aeternum* . . .
Medea in the doghouse . . .

WHAT THEN IS THE HIERARCHY
OF TORTURES . . .
My unkind kin
where have they vanished to shatter . . .
Let us consider seeking
among the ruins
on the peristyle of . . .

The Man with the Telephone (*entering stage left, his clothing torn*)
Are you looking for something . . .

Marie S.
The secret of Mercy
The succour of Vengeance . . .
The slough of Tears . . .

The Man with the Telephone
I was just passing
and I said to myself
that I may
quite unambiguously
lend a hand in your search . . .

Marie S.
Alas . . . 'I was searching for a fool when I found you' . . .
Everything disjoins, contorts
and capsizes . . .

Pause.

Where then are your hands . . .

The Man with the Telephone
You were right to give in . . .
Giving in was the unbeatable way out . . .

Marie S.
I, a defeatist . . . a sequacious . . .
'You did not yield one inch' . . .
My Amazons are crying out . . .
My winged Centaurs are lullabying me . . .

Pause.

The Man with the Telephone (*groaning*)
Your rapier-dragging drunkard
had the nerve to decree
a day of fasting
a day of prayer . . .
Unanimously voted in
by the Senate . . .

Marie S.
Is that the reason
for this beggar's disguise
for these sobs of a pimp . . .

The Man with the Telephone
We are all beggars . . .
nepotistic . . . stateless . . . intruders . . .
criminals . . . traitors . . .
I must imperatively halt here . . .

Marie S.
Courteous destroyer
putting an end
is forthwith frightful . . .

The Man with the Telephone
Where are your children . . .

Marie S.
Pilgrims . . .
Peregrines on earth . . .

The Man with the Telephone (*approaching*)
Then you shall . . . take this hand . . .

Marie S. *takes it. Her hands become stained with blood.*

Marie S. (*jubilant*)
Shall I recognise you
As my fellow creature
As my placental Double
As a twin . . .

The Man with the Telephone
When, then . . . tell me
WHEN . . .

Marie S. (*making as if to go, laughing*)
Would you have refrained from sinking
your canine teeth into the Mountain
to rediscover the salty source of your eyes . . .
to untwine the Möbius strip . . .

The Man with the Telephone
HALT, Marie S. . . . HALT . . .
Look at my hands . . .
Here IT IS
the BLOOD of your KIN . . .

Marie S. (*covering her face with her bloody hands*)
. . . Treacherous . . . ill-bred dog . . .
Eye without heart . . .
'I am dying from not dying' . . .

The Man with the Telephone (*hysterically*)
You did disobey time and again . . .
It will be . . .
technically feasible
to resuscitate you
to force you to kneel
to seduce you . . .

Marie S. (*exultantly*)
TOO LATE . . .
the Seraglio's cruelty
has abandoned its obese machine of war . . .
Never again will one gorge oneself
with the bloody nectar of one's victims . . .

The Man with the Telephone
You are blinded by ignorance, MADAM . . .
Have you forgotten your OWN ORDERS . . .

Marie S.
Unfortunate FOOL . . . Affable angel . . .
'No one has the right to obey' . . .

The Man with the Telephone
THE RIGHT, MY CHILD
THE RIGHT EYE
HAS THE MISFORTUNE
OF BEING THE BROTHER OF THE LEFT EYE!

A blinding light suddenly floods the stage. A violent wind begins to blow.

Marie S.
VOICE OF SHAMELESSNESS
MY BROTHER
WHAT HAVE YOU DONE . . .
YOU HURLED ME
TO THE CRIPPLED CROWN
OF THE WORLD!

A black storm of burnt papers plunges the stage into darkness.

This page intentionally left blank

Methuen Drama Student Editions

This page intentionally left blank

Methuen Drama Modern Plays

include work by

Edward Albee
Jean Anouilh
John Arden
Margaretta D'Arcy
Peter Barnes
Sebastian Barry
Brendan Behan
Dermot Bolger
Edward Bond
Bertolt Brecht
Howard Brenton
Anthony Burgess
Simon Burke
Jim Cartwright
Caryl Churchill
Noël Coward
Lucinda Coxon
Sarah Daniels
Nick Darke
Nick Dear
Shelagh Delaney
David Edgar
David Eldridge
Dario Fo
Michael Frayn
John Godber
Paul Godfrey
David Greig
John Guare
Peter Handke
David Harrower
Jonathan Harvey
Iain Heggie
Declan Hughes
Terry Johnson
Sarah Kane
Charlotte Keatley
Barrie Keeffe
Howard Korder

Robert Lepage
Doug Lucie
Martin McDonagh
John McGrath
Terrence McNally
David Mamet
Patrick Marber
Arthur Miller
Mtwa, Ngema & Simon
Tom Murphy
Phyllis Nagy
Peter Nichols
Sean O'Brien
Joseph O'Connor
Joe Orton
Louise Page
Joe Penhall
Luigi Pirandello
Stephen Poliakoff
Franca Rame
Mark Ravenhill
Philip Ridley
Reginald Rose
Willy Russell
Jean-Paul Sartre
Sam Shepard
Wole Soyinka
Simon Stephens
Shelagh Stephenson
Peter Straughan
C. P. Taylor
Theatre de Complicite
Theatre Workshop
Sue Townsend
Judy Upton
Timberlake Wertenbaker
Roy Williams
Snoo Wilson
Victoria Wood

This page intentionally left blank

Methuen Drama Contemporary Dramatists

include

John Arden (two volumes)
Arden & D'Arcy
Peter Barnes (three volumes)
Sebastian Barry
Dermot Bolger
Edward Bond (eight volumes)
Howard Brenton
    (two volumes)
Richard Cameron
Jim Cartwright
Caryl Churchill
    (two volumes)
Sarah Daniels (two volumes)
Nick Darke
David Edgar (three volumes)
David Eldridge
Ben Elton
Dario Fo (two volumes)
Michael Frayn (three volumes)
John Godber (three volumes)
Paul Godfrey
David Greig
John Guare
Lee Hall (two volumes)
Peter Handke
Jonathan Harvey
    (two volumes)
Declan Hughes
Terry Johnson (three volumes)
Sarah Kane
Barrie Keeffe
Bernard-Marie Koltès
    (two volumes)
David Lan
Bryony Lavery
Deborah Levy
Doug Lucie

David Mamet (four volumes)
Martin McDonagh
Duncan McLean
Anthony Minghella
    (two volumes)
Tom Murphy (five volumes)
Phyllis Nagy
Anthony Neilson
Philip Osment
Gary Owen
Louise Page
Stewart Parker (two volumes)
Joe Penhall
Stephen Poliakoff
    (three volumes)
David Rabe
Mark Ravenhill
Christina Reid
Philip Ridley
Willy Russell
Eric-Emmanuel Schmitt
Ntozake Shange
Sam Shepard (two volumes)
Wole Soyinka (two volumes)
Simon Stephens
Shelagh Stephenson
David Storey (three volumes)
Sue Townsend
Judy Upton
Michel Vinaver
    (two volumes)
Arnold Wesker (two volumes)
Michael Wilcox
Roy Williams (two volumes)
Snoo Wilson (two volumes)
David Wood (two volumes)
Victoria Wood

This page intentionally left blank

Methuen Drama World Classics

include

Jean Anouilh (two volumes)
Brendan Behan
Aphra Behn
Bertolt Brecht (eight volumes)
Büchner
Bulgakov
Calderón
Čapek
Anton Chekhov
Noël Coward (eight volumes)
Feydeau
Eduardo De Filippo
Max Frisch
John Galsworthy
Gogol
Gorky (two volumes)
Harley Granville Barker
  (two volumes)
Victor Hugo
Henrik Ibsen (six volumes)
Jarry

Lorca (three volumes)
Marivaux
Mustapha Matura
David Mercer (two volumes)
Arthur Miller (five volumes)
Molière
Musset
Peter Nichols (two volumes)
Joe Orton
A. W. Pinero
Luigi Pirandello
Terence Rattigan
  (two volumes)
W. Somerset Maugham
  (two volumes)
August Strindberg
  (three volumes)
J. M. Synge
Ramón del Valle-Inclan
Frank Wedekind
Oscar Wilde

This page intentionally left blank

Methuen Drama Classical Greek Dramatists

include

Aeschylus Plays: One
(Persians, Seven Against Thebes, Suppliants,
Prometheus Bound)

Aeschylus Plays: Two
(Oresteia: Agamemnon, Libation-Bearers, Eumenides)

Aristophanes Plays: One
(Acharnians, Knights, Peace, Lysistrata)

Aristophanes Plays: Two
(Wasps, Clouds, Birds, Festival Time, Frogs)

Aristophanes & Menander: New Comedy
(Women in Power, Wealth, The Malcontent,
The Woman from Samos)

Euripides Plays: One
(Medea, The Phoenician Women, Bacchae)

Euripides Plays: Two
(Hecuba, The Women of Troy,
Iphigeneia at Aulis, Cyclops)

Euripides Plays: Three
(Alkestis, Helen, Ion)

Euripides Plays: Four
(Elektra, Orestes, Iphigeneia in Tauris)

Euripides Plays: Five
(Andromache, Herakles' Children, Herakles)

Euripides Plays: Six
(Hippolytos, Suppliants, Rhesos)

Sophocles Plays: One
(Oedipus the King, Oedipus at Colonus, Antigone)

Sophocles Plays: Two
(Ajax, Women of Trachis, Electra, Philoctetes)

For a complete catalogue
of Methuen Drama titles
write to:

Methuen Drama
A & C Black Publishers Limited
38 Soho Square
London W1D 3HB

or you can visit our website at
www.acblack.com

Printed in the USA
CPSIA information can be obtained
at www.ICGtesting.com
LVHW020852171024
794056LV00002B/496

9 781408 103920